Advance Praise for

Wintering

"Megan Snyder-Camp makes a daring entrance into history, first in the winter camp of Lewis and Clark, whose 'days slide through my hands like rope.' In lyrical prose that adapts the form and traditional journey of the haibun, the poet juxtaposes the explorers' mapping and journals with her own contemporary life. Native Americans come to the fore in a second haibun, which leads to a third in which the author goes east in search of the lost 'Indian vocabularies' the explorers collected. The book ends with an essay about the surprising results of that search. What lingers most is the remarkable poetic experience of being in the past and present at once, 'never just one path taken,' but 'five paths . . . taken at once, fingering out their hopeless green.'"

—Martha Collins

"Snyder-Camp weaves genres and concepts in an intriguing and open-ended examination of national and personal American mythology. In her lyrical analysis of the Lewis and Clark expedition, she maintains a perceptive lens—'without its story, the images are gorgeous' notes the writer, and proceeds to make space for both the lush beauties and the stark atrocities of history."

—Laura Da'

"*Wintering* is a ceremonial feast of a book, its offerings rich in language that is both lyrical and scholarly. Snyder-Camp restores the washed-out textbook myth of the explorers' arrival at the Pacific to its vibrancy, a *human* story as sorrowful, terrifying, foolish, exhausting, culpable, and occasionally funny as all our lives are, if truly told. Snyder-Camp tells truly here of the 'voyage of distances' that we, all of us, by turns create and attempt to cross."

—Melinda Mueller

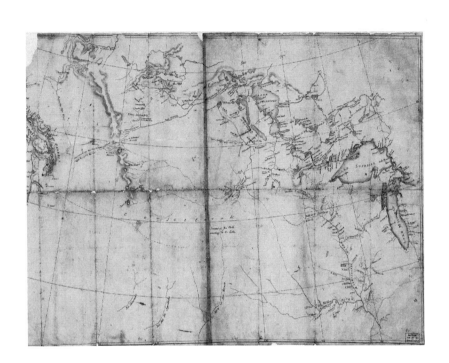

Wintering

Megan Snyder-Camp

TUPELO PRESS
North Adams, Massachusetts

Library of Congress Cataloging-in-Publication Data available upon request.
ISBN: 978-1-936797-70-7

Cover and text designed by Dede Cummings.
Cover: Collaged images include a fragment of a vocabulary docu-ment collected by Meriwether Lewis for Thomas Jefferson, courtesy of the American Philosophical Society in Philadelphia; photograph by Megan Snyder-Camp; and a section of a Corps of Discovery map, with annotations in brown ink by Meriwether Lewis. Pen and ink. 1803(?). Used with permission of Art Resource.

First paperback edition: August 2016.

Tupelo Press
P.O. Box 1767, North Adams, Massachusetts 01247
Telephone: (413) 664–9611 / editor@tupelopress.org
www.tupelopress.org

Tupelo Press is an award-winning independent literary press that publishes fine fiction, nonfiction, and poetry in books that are a joy to hold as well as read. Tupelo Press is a registered 501(c)(3) non-profit organization, and we rely on public support to carry out our mission of publishing extraordinary work that may be outside the realm of the large commercial publishers. Financial donations are welcome and are tax deductible.

for TJ

How much of the stuff in the fort is real?

Everything, except for the meat, is real, but not
from the expedition,
or that time.

—FROM THE FAQS PAGE FOR THE RESTORED FORT CLATSOP,
LEWIS AND CLARK NATIONAL HISTORICAL PARK,
ON THE NATIONAL PARK SERVICE WEBSITE

Contents

Preface

IN NOVEMBER 2009, pregnant with my second child, I began studying Meriwether Lewis and William Clark's arrival at the Pacific. I wanted to know about these explorers who in November 1805 had come here—to the Northwest that I love and now call home—miserable, wary, and frightened.

On my first visit to Lewis and Clark's trail, I spent a month in a borrowed house on Washington's Long Beach peninsula, near where the explorers had wintered. My husband and two-year-old joined me for most of that time, and I decided not to erase their voices from the travelogue I was keeping. Reading Lewis and Clark's journals alongside Matsuo Bashō's *Narrow Road to the Interior,* I admired the seventeenth-century Japanese poet's ability to carry two tracks of imagery at once—the observed landscape and an interior one—as he traveled. He didn't travel with a two-year-old, though, which felt to me less like two tracks running than like a cloud of asterisks. But Bashō's haibun form, with its fragments of prose and poetry, offered me the form I needed to map where I was, which was often several places at once.

That November turned out to be the first of three Novembers in which I sent myself out in the explorers' wake, drawn to the gaps I found in accounts of the expedition and its aftermath. As I got my bearings, I found myself lingering where many historians had hurried past: sites of absence, of error, of silence.

I have tried to be careful and respectful of what is not mine, while at the same time not remaining silent when I stumbled across a toxic area of scholarly erasure. I've come to see this as a project about—and against—distance. When Meriwether Lewis was angry with his Clatsop neighbors, he wrote, "I treated them with great distance." When Thomas Jefferson was angry with one of his slaves, his practice was to sell the man to a new owner living as far away as possible, creating an impossible distance between the man and his family, his community. I think of the gaps in our stories as distances.

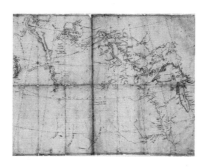

"the Skelleton of this monster
on the Sand"

To create the distance a frontier demands.

Green hunger splitting the husk of our lives.

The husk turned from.

To seek out that turning, that distance.

To set it loose just to see what it does. To watch it learn to walk.

To build a home beside it.

With what wood we found.

Through the fog we tail a milk truck painted with puns—
The Udder Guys, Dairy Aire—then half a house on a
flatbed. You're trying to explain the difference between
tension and piecework, a small aggravation inside a larger
sadness. Our son sleeps in the backseat and our daughter,
not yet born, turns inside me. Briefly, cut from the fog,

a field strewn with mower parts, spools, then a lull of grass,
six crooked graves. The half house turns left and we double
our speed.

The river has rose nearly 8 Inches to day
and has every appearance of a tide,
from what Cause I can't Say—

When Clark pointed at individual Indians within a group hoping to learn their names, he kept getting the same answer. A new edition of the journals tells us in a footnote those Indians were saying, He is pointing at him. The road to the winter camp the explorers chose for its ready elk is now marked with a yellow sign warning ELK. Sometimes

they would name a bird twice, three times, tongues lapping the fog. This winter of naming spread and battened in like a quilt: what they remembered and what they kept trying to see. They built the fort out of anger at the constant damp, the wet rolling logs that had frightened them now bound into thick-walled rooms, or cut for fire. But whether to trust

the first draft of the journals, or the third . . . Reading interviews with writers, I notice their answers are longer and smarter than a decade ago. Even though on the page writers still settle in at a kitchen table with tape recorder and cigarettes, through the smooth arch of their syntax it's clear they've actually written out their replies, revised them, rather than hear their own stutter transcribed.

Upstairs my son sings every song he knows, retells whole conversations against the sleep I've laid out. Every day he throws the cup of his words like dice. Like Lewis, who broke a months-long silence to write about a beaver he saw, H was mesmerized by the one he spotted this morning at the fort. Everything after it either a littler beaver or a bigger

one. So an idea is smoothed, built to its socket and tested, rather than battering the shore like a slick log until it lodges or splits. *Dismal Nitch*: the men balanced all night on the turning blackness.

Whether or not there was a bear seems beside the point. When Patrick Gass, one of the explorers, published his journals in 1807—seven years ahead of Lewis and Clark— the in-house illustrator back east etched his best guess of a grizzly: a beautiful, shaggy ten-foot dog with the explorer tiny and trembling in a tree just overhead. I don't believe

one thing leads to another. I don't believe Rukeyser, who says choice after choice falls away. I believe in the hung mobile: the tether and each animal's idle spin, its surface the reflection of its surface. Today I drive farther north than the explorers ventured—Clark started up this peninsula but after four miles of what he named Long Beach, declared

the beach before him the same as the beach behind him. I drive to the tip, Leadbetter Point. The water on both sides comes nearly to the road, and at the end I can hear the water breathing, the opening of a thousand eyes along the shore. Tiny water birds stationed just beyond the waves float dully. So small I first thought they were their young.

In the clearing a cell phone signal delivers two old messages from friends, one about to give birth, one at a tearful dinner. No, never just one path taken; five paths are taken at once, fingering out their hopeless green. How grateful I am whenever I come to a clearing like this one.

The wind
which is the cause of our delay,
does not retard the motions of those people at all

Rain and wind continue but the leaves hold to the trees, some stubbornness that summer must have set. The three of us are on our way to Altoona, where the explorers either saw the ocean or didn't. The spot from which they wrote "Ocian in view!" doesn't offer an ocean view, and so historians agreed the explorers were mistaken. The new

theory is that the ocean has since moved out of sight. You ask, again, why you hardly ever appear in my poems. I've been trying to understand these men's desire to map the wilderness, to see anything but the sorrow their marking makes. Is it any different how writers stumble out to the desk before dawn, hoping to startle up the heart? What I

love most I mean to leave be. Every day I call my poems off you and lead them back to the trail. We pass crows and the occasional black cow. H receives his apple whole, two-handed, delivers each bite like a pin to a map. Though time and again what I mean to shelter flies up.

So long anxious to See

The dead-end road is six miles long. An empty-handed hunter walks to his truck, on which someone has pasted a NO HUNTING sign. The road repeats this prohibition over and over, though everyone we pass wears orange. Today's road narrows to a single thought, and a man walks alone with a rake. On our right the river comes close, tongues

at the road's edge, and one rain-bright lawn offers a set of three swings on a riverward tilt, so that the children must rest their weight on one hip or the other, depending on whether they prefer the river or the road.

and the roreing or noise
made by the waves brakeing on the rockey Shores
(as I Suppose) may be heard

The river a yellow-gray impossibility, the sign tentative in
its claim to the explorers' camp. Somewhere near here, a
few miles perhaps, this spot from which they saw the ocean
or did not. All the shore lined with young trees. Our son
another tree, pocketing the tiny pinecones that scrabble in
the wind. This time I've gotten the day right and we're here

on the day they were here, but today following their path
feels more distant than staying home and reading their
journals: I can't imagine myself alongside them, can't
imagine why they kept moving forward. I'm nervous when
H climbs all the way to the top tunnel of the McDonald's
PlayPlace where we stop for lunch. The other mother there

has four children, who lead H up and coax him down.
They're used to these fears. The mother says every morning
she releases them into one room or another; they've driven
half an hour for this one in which we can barely hear their
calls through the tubing and the hammer of rain against the
windows. One explorer, the boy George Shannon, was lost

twice along the route, separated from the others for days at
a time, and both times as he slept by a river he was found.
H, I notice, is never sad about the same thing twice, though
his handful of fears stays constant. There are two windows
above our borrowed bed, offering thin slices of the same
pine. Three walls of bare drywall, streaks of paint from
paintings that are gone.

No streetlights here, no moon. I can hear geese, and sometimes a car a mile or two away. We can't find a flashlight in our borrowed house. Once a car pulled onto the beach behind us, turned its headlights off, and raced past. We heard it everywhere, turning, and I made us stand in the water until it drove away. Today I finger the split

of my days, the mind of mothering and the mind of poems. Outside the air is still. Water bells the lichen on a fir tree. The wood beams of this room have loosed their knots and stand open-jawed. I am afraid of loss as I have never been.

water passing with great velocity forming & boiling in a most horriable manner

The explorers row past a single, tremendous pillar of basalt in the river, though for days they won't write of it. The black rock, origin of the last recorded myth of a tribe dead of smallpox, now carved to hold a radio tower. Either to put words down on paper is to map: tuning the radio, you hear

in the darkness something coming, warning. Or writing is creation, and I am the fool holding open the door.

I turn the heat on and watch the gulls fly backward in the wind through the beaten grasses of the empty lots. I'm reminded of the days before H's birth, when I wanted nothing more than to undo the latch, escape. Art of the body, the body trembling, tethered. In the Bitterroot Mountains the horse carrying Clark's wooden desk

stumbled and fell forty yards down the mountainside. The horse survived but the desk was destroyed. Here they begin to eat candles, or candlefish, depending on the editor. The whiskey is gone, and the salt, while slim native canoes and water birds bob gracefully, relentlessly, toward them. Lewis goes mad with what is daily taken from him; Clark

tries again to describe the salal's shine. This morning workers are cutting down the tuliptree in my borrowed meadow and moving the aspen from over the septic into the tuliptree's socket. After lunch the view will be different though I will not have moved.

the only wood we could get to burn
on this little Island on which we have encamped
is the newly discovered
Ash, which makes a tolerable fire

The explorers had hoped to meet a ship here to save them from walking the miles home, and there were two—a Russian freighter and the *Lydia*, a trading ship from Boston—but the explorers didn't see them. The peninsula has named itself the Graveyard of the Pacific and sells annual posters tallying shipwrecks. Boys fish from the half-

sunk hulls, and at lunch the locals drive onto the sand. By the dunes a sea lion, yesterday's, eyes toward the sea bulging. He appears line-drawn, his short fur jagged across stretching skin. The flies attending him barely look up. Overhead a gull calls out, the clouds change, and the morning's storm holds its tongue. On Tuesday a man washed up, one of a couple trying to sail to Hawaii in a twenty-five-footer.

In this winter, the explorers produced more drawings—of canoes they envied, of the Nez Perce practice of head-flattening, of trees, of the condor whose head they carried back—than in any other season of their journey. Today's newspaper tells of a Spanish painter whose only figurative piece was a self-portrait as a young man, holding a sketch

of another body. All other years he painted only still lifes in which heavy cantaloupes, bread, wooden boxes loom from tiny canvases. The critic notes he was a master of the dry, the porous, the nonreflective, but when shine was needed the painter affixed gleam "as from a price gun."

our Small Canoe
which got Seperated in the fog this morning
joined us this evening

More rain today, enough that H cries for the end of our hike. I meant to see where Sacagawea finally met the ocean, where the whale—*the Skelleton of this monster on the Sand*—had washed up. On a trail above the beach H hides from me inside the belly of a cedar, and after a spark of lightning we run down the muddy slope to our car. H

falls asleep to "Pink Moon" as you drive us to the cabin, water making its way down everything, ferns upon ferns narrowing the road, old evergreens picketing the ocean view. The sea and its edits. Onto a road middled green and reaching for our car, up the cliff to a cabin with a purple sun painted across the side. But at the cabin is another car,

and in the cabin another family. I've remembered our reservation wrong and am a day late, and so what would've been ours isn't. We turn back, follow the highway north again, pulling into every viewpoint to try to stamp a shorthand of the trip onto our day. One of the three rocks along the coast is historically important, but which?

All three rise from the ocean with "rounded but sharpened" tops. H sleeps in the car, and the rain has lightened. You ask about weightlessness. An hour later, at the pizza parlor in town, H watches a hunting video game, but just the beginning, where deer, foxes, lions, giraffes, and elephants cross the screen. Without its story the images are gorgeous.

the Skelleton of this monster on the Sand

When word of the whale came, Sacagawea argued with her husband, and then with Clark, to join the group of men going to see. She carried her fourteen-month-old son, or did not—the records do not say—down the rocky slope to the sea and sat an hour by the cleaned skeleton. It was, Clark noted, the only time she asked him for anything.

Unbroken sun burning the water from the trees. I walk on a sand trail following deer tracks. The birds are quiet. A hundred yards from the shore the trail is abruptly, deeply flooded, bordered by high grass and low trees. For what will our daughter blame us? The explorers waste this sunny, calm morning on ceremony. They sit on the beach,

unpacking the fine clothes they brought to wear that last westward mile. Sashes, hats, and regimental coats are pulled from the wet bags, dried, smoothed. This proud delay costs them almost a week: a sudden hard rain is followed by a flood tide which pens them on the narrow, log-splintering beach for five days. Remnants of a crab

claw, remnants of a gull's wing. Steam rises off brown ferns. Along the bay whole columns of birds move in every direction: the fast, papery ones, the heavier fish-divers, a lone black heron. The paper birds touch every scrap of air, leave it.

one man Shannon Set out early
to walk on the Island
to kill Something

At the cove where the explorers finally touched the ocean, small black nuts tangle into nets. Nests. The waves foam and stick, some rising into colored snow: an algae bloom miles away. One side of the shore walled with smooth boulders, the other guarded by driftwood and a few sharp rocks carved with tunnels and chutes the sea has made.

I've forgotten my notebook again, and so let the minutes fall. Today's horoscope says I'm ambitious but not trust-worthy. We've been to Cape Disappointment five times now, PlayPlace three. With each return I lay our days more steadily on each other. The explorers' days slide through my hands like rope. At first I was glad to follow

them into the rain but now I want only to test that wall between the arrival and the return. Is this because I'm pregnant again? My mind both fixed inside the days and casting into the dark. Interested not in the path of water across a nation but in the work of water on stone, the work of days on words.

Symmetrical geography:
that the land, folded, would clasp.

If I keep many small notebooks, if I rise at four, will my days carry like rope? During the journey, Lewis collected at least twenty-three Indian vocabularies for Jefferson, who spent thirty years sending men out to collect Indian words, never finding what he wanted. The grammar too strange. At the end of his presidency, he had the words' dead weight

shipped home.

Lewis abandoned his journal for months as they approached the Pacific and settled on its edge, and when he resumed in the new year, thick-tongued in the camp of moccasins and salt, he spoke only of the plants and birds he half remembered. Fern by fern he filled the pages. Now an herbarium in Philadelphia protects these cuttings.

when cloves are not to be had
use double the quantity of Allspice,
and when no spice can be obtained
use the bark of the root of sausafras;
when sperits can not be had
use oil stone of the beaver reduce it to a stif past

Today refuses to open. I search the local bookstore in vain for that Frost poem with the two halves barely joined. Some houses here fill their front windows with a lattice of colored sea glass bottles, emptiness transfigured.

By now the explorers, subsisting on dog meat, are barely
speaking to the natives, writing instead of the safety of their
winter fort, how high and how red the wood. In the parking
lot, the driver for Strange Landscape Services stares up at
the sky. "You see that V," he says. "Sideways, more like a
jaw?" I drive two towns over to visit the shipwreck

museum. The forty-foot lifeboat self-righting, self-bailing,
at practice through the window, throwing the body out and
out again. Oscar, they call the body. Coffeepot chained to
the wall. An older couple kisses beneath a model whaling
boat carved in whalebone. In gillnetting there's only the
floater and the diver; the practice of seining has ended

but here are beautiful sepia photos of horses straining to
haul every living thing onto shore. Driving back, I stop at
the ocean. Low tide, hail, gulls thrown like seeds. A county
truck pulls up alongside something half sunk in the sand,
then drives on. At the house I find H mesmerized by a
video clip of a panda sneezing. We watch the panda sneeze
ten times, twenty. The sun sets behind three walls of
clouds, and behind me it's already night.

in walking on the Sand after crossing the river

I Saw a Singular Species of fish
which I had never before Seen
one of the men Call this fish a Skaite,

it is properly a Thornback.

No rain all morning. I keep trying to take new paths but find myself at the same junctures, realizing too late that the path I'm on is the one that's flooded at the end. How differently the mind moves in a familiar place. So today I see the crab-shell fragments and wait for the gull's wing. Today Lewis went to the ocean alone and didn't write of it,

except to carve his name on a tree. Tomorrow Clark will go, and the others over the next few days, until the edge of the forest is netted in names. Calm of the water-lifted vocabularies. Those early weeks after H was born, our home was a winter fort in which you and I spoke always of sleep. By sleep we meant love, and the beforelife, and the

power we could not seem to shake down from our sleeves. We spoke so quietly of sleep no one heard us, not the baby, and often not each other. Over that long winter the explorers sewed 338 pairs of moccasins, boiled 28 gallons of salt from the sea, stood sentry, and named everything they could see, or remembered seeing. One by one they begged for home.

In consequence of the clouds this evening
I lost my P. M. observation for Equal Altitudes,
and from the same cause

have not been able to take a single observation
since we have been at this place.
nothing extraordinary happened today.

The beginning protected from sight. The beginning licking its plate. These men had such trouble telling their story after they returned, though they could hardly talk about anything else. Years of revision left only these scraps, in unevenly revised triplicate, which we now call complete.

Wind all last night, and this morning the car shaking, another storm coming. Already the roads are furred with smaller branches, and the sand at the ocean is softening.

it is true we Could travel
even now on our return as far

as the timbered Country reaches,
or to the falls of the river,
but further it would be madness

Hundreds of geese arrive in clusters from the north, working against the wind to land on the bay's mud flats. The RV that has been slowly moving around the peninsula the past few days passes by again, then heads toward the oyster shop. The wind is loud with what it carries.

and even were we happily over those plains
and in the woodey countrey
at the foot of the rockey mountains,

we could not possibly pass
that emence bearier of mountains

untill the drift wood comes down in the Spring
and lodges on the Shore &c.

Driving through the arms of giant cedars downed in last
night's storm, I pass men sawing waist-high trunks in half
and trucks snowplowing them aside to make a red, raw
gate. Everywhere limbs, moss, small interruptions and
chatter cover the road. Finally the forest is everywhere
as all the small branches and greenery soften both lanes.

I drive to the beach where the explorers finally met the
Pacific, just after a storm like this one. A wet gravel trail
rises through marshes to the shore, where black sand, foam,
two bald eagles, and dozens of gulls circle over what the
storm released. Tree after tree upturned in the surf, rinsed
plain. And the sand drawn up around everything that rested

on its surface, so that each shadow is a body of its own. This
particular joy. A jar of whole pickles, a short frame of light,
the day broken open by what moves past it. All along this
coast driftwood—though that word is too calm for what
has been done to it—pared to the top knuckle of roots.

it is true we Could travel
even now

When I'd asked at the ranger station what Lewis and Clark had seen, the ranger would only say that the shore is no longer where it was, so the viewpoint wouldn't have the view you want. Every year, to support the jetties, they dredge hundreds of tons of sand from the river and haul it here, and from here it returns to the river.

but further it would be madness

Tonight all is silent at the end of the peninsula that Clark won't reach. Nor will he cross the mile-wide spit to discover the bay, or living along it the wintering families whose empty summer village he tore apart. Instead let them sleep another year, let their numbers not yet be counted nor

their words lain open like fish on the table. I empty my rented cabin and throw the *I Ching*, which comes up *listen; listen; abysmal water.*

The Fort

Labor

later the sound
of my own voice was a way across
tally of minutes and reprieve narrowing as the neighbor

mowing framed in
in in as he pushed across his small slope
his apple tree all blossom

grass bag filling
I watched from my chair the math
and winch of my body opening she in darkness I in daylight

Hive Boxes

Walking   the   baby   at   noon   along   our   vacation   road

[   ]

ryegrass salvia thistle wild distance folding six white boxes'

[   ]

nearly colliding but clearer, wouldn't) not mine the hum I was

[   ]

here not to disappear my poems waiting in the city upturning

[   ]

the   pasture's   cold   green   body.   Someone   else's   work

someone's split panic the hive splitting into mother and mind

[   ]

Guide to Avian Architecture

What we built to hold us, the year's memory,
menus and daytrips, after a while

came loose. Those nights
we balanced on each other's mistakes,

cradling our wine:
twigs those branches now.

Who knew what lived there?
She she she called one bird.

What lived there knew its place.
Another bird splits its nest wide,

hinges the gap with spider silk, learning
to give, to give, to give until breaking. Only then—

either one gives until breaking or one does not.

Pastoral

We turned our grief out to graze,
gave over the year's tender greening

across those slabbed hills, sharp haunches
pressing down the field, what pain, what good

taken down to its root, the root taken, each green spear
until the year itself was consumed, driven back to the mud

it had once been. When they turned with patient hunger toward us,
these warm beasts, rib-hull, pine-hull—it had been their course

we followed, their lead across the distance.
Others chose philosophy, we heard,

or prayer. But we were the only ones
who lasted through the winter, we who offered up

our homes and our crops and everything we had once dared to build.
We knew it was the store and depth and cover

from rain we had given our grief—how we'd grown
to love the damp heat above even what we remembered

of each other—that in turn fed us
what little we could take.

where is my love where is his phone cord where is his song
he is gone from this sunny day has taken the kids back home
for when I get done with where I am the cedars
I can see the men took turns carving their names
but surely it has risen they took a boat back took the whiskey
                                                    and the little
crackers shaped like fish my love is waiting or not waiting I
cannot identify the birds the cries not mine to soothe these years
I have waited to love him better or if it has not risen it is
somewhere in the sea beneath us becoming everything else

Ozette

After a while the 500-year-old village became a secret, carved into the wall of the forest where it met the Pacific, eleven long houses and their racks of drying fish, their dogs. No roads to this town, only boats and the memory of boaters. Blankets made from woodpecker feathers, cattail fluff, cedar bark and dog hair woven into a plaid pattern.

At least that's what I remember of the museum's diorama. When the mud came down the mountain and covered the village, no one had lived there for years. It was a boater who remembered, after a while, that the village was gone, and also that it had once existed. Archaeologists brought garden hoses to wash the mud off and hooked the hoses up

to the sea. Some of what had been preserved in the mud was destroyed that day by the water pressure, and then later most else was ruined by the wind and rain, but at least for a few weeks they could hold the bones in their hands. The archaeologists brought their dogs, they lived there a while.

Sandy (Quicksand) River

Where the explorers waited in their boats for water,
paid reenactors now flatten marsh grass, now stop their ears

against the journals' mention of geese.
Saw a Small Crab-apple with all the taste & flavor

of the common—
Those Indians were all armed with Pistols

or bows and arrows ready Sprung war axes &c.
Indians continue to be with us, Several Canoes

Continue with us. Across the margin
my shadow. A day overwriting the next,

a life: cranberries, a clearing, my daughter
turning in the crib. Reach freed of its root.

Clark at Cape Disappointment

When we turned from river to sea,
we came to a town whose houses

stood empty. No dead, no gardens.
We entered as through water,

taking hold of the strongest walls and splitting them
to fit our shelter for the night.

Fire. *My servent danced.*
Impossible to sleep

in the carved beds we found, winter already
and the rain a code come loose.

Abundance

Maple, slick–ewe, birchbark, lapis, eelgrass, red rock,
grouse, swan, the island so thick with migrating geese

Clark couldn't sleep. The forest so thick with cedar
Lewis couldn't see. The river so swift-turning,

the fish and the tide and the pebbled extra
of their looking, the seeking-notes echoed back,

the sprawl in which new names were made
for pages and pages of what purpled

and split-finned and dried, the best chaptered out
into wooden cases sent back east. Eight seasons

unhooked from their loves such as would ruin a man,
did ruin the men—that life now shy thimble-furls

in its greenhouse safe above Philadelphia.
Slow green from their very seeds, the scissored reach

for whatever staggered into bloom, into view,
across their path. Sap rising to the juncture

of each new name, forgotten stalk
stubbornly curing the cut, loss thickened against return.

At the Experimental Forest

Clearcut, tenure, snow
where the reservoir is.
In the hall of photos, each man

alone on his slope,
smiling up from the muddy question.

◆

Here the logjam broke in the '96 flood. Scientists filmed
the churning of rock on rock. Tall cedars along the bank
ground into shards. When the fragments are a particular
size—when they are small enough—they rise to the
surface and float out to sea.

◆

In the lost and found, a box of notebooks. One asked about
fire. One asked about the weight of birds. One asked if all
were lost and a record kept.

The first to arrive were the trees. Second, the wood wreck of an Asian fishing boat: 1,700 years ago the slick black prow. 600 years ago a Spanish galleon. Its metal bent into fish hooks, joiners. Its metal all that remains (the placard says) of the tribe who found it.

◆

Lewis and Clark survived on what they named arrow-root while building the winter fort. Locked it against what ran wild. If to speak is to call up what lies buried, who can blame Lewis for his silence? In the rain, in the wilderness of his own mind, Lewis named everything. Green green green: these lives bending and dividing. Multiplying.

◆

green of fir green of cedar
green of yew green of hemlock
green of the vine green of the air
through moss green scarf waving
from each tree green to the river
green that falls across it
green that everywhere has fallen
green like a fishing net
green our hands upon it

The pristine wilderness, the untouched plains, the thousand thousand buffalo, the countless bears that Lewis and Clark saw: what looked like abundance was actually absence. Decades before the explorers set out, the smallpox virus swept ahead of them, back and forth across the land until many tribes had been reduced to a small band of survivors. The animals they'd hunted roamed free and multiplied, the land grew thick around them, and passing through, you could be forgiven for saying you had found Eden. Were not those survivors now your guides.

◆

Copper and salt: the winter
I stretch again and again over me.

◆

A grid of short trails unfurling. Tiny flags and hoods nearly touching. Within each frame a scattering of metal boxes. Stuck foil. Tape. So your poems, said the British geologist, there are no people in them?

In one part of the forest, cedars, dying, breathe through tubes. I had tried to find the waterfalls, tried to speak to the woman at the country store, tried to watch the light on the river. Where the cedars lay was a carpet. All on the carpet

was slowly becoming carpet. I was afraid to remain in one place. I walked a thin path around the cedars, past and up a slight hill where there was still only silence. Two cut logs: a desk and a chair. I sat and nothing in the forest moved.

Even my life vanished.

Last night, reading, I heard the geologist tapping on my window. For your poem, he said. Outside, the moon near full. As my eyes adjusted I saw a faint white circle etched in the sky, so wide the cedars nearly hid it. A hoop for the moon, a saucer. Spill of its yellow milk. Or say it happened

this way instead, without the geologist: I was bringing toilet paper from the car when the night sky lightened. Arms of white, I saw where the moon, like a leashed dog, had paced its dark yard bare.

I walked in the body of the whale, up-curved branches ribbing over me, exhalations of small spores, steam. The river a long way down. All held still and seemed free of other lives. Here a yellow coral, there a charcoal trunk. Nothing rolled down the hill. The river and the sky were equally far and often I mistook spiraling leaves for birds.

Where the path turned to shale I turned back. For my son I pocketed a green translucent snail-shell, for my daughter a knuckle of cedar. No bones, no bones. Just the careful green lives.

♦

I can no longer hold the explorers' days inside my own. Terrible rain at the center of their November is, this year, just sun. Burn piles. Small brown birds I can't name, frost-weighted leaves falling like stones. Traps and jugs and flags: the work goes on while the scientists sleep, or while I do. This morning frost silvered our little clearing, and as morning went on our roofs gave off steam. A van of college students studying epiphytes idles in the lot. Later, the kids fill ice trays from the river. Whatever they are called swims.

The Indian Vocabularies

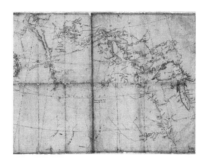

Too late for the tour, I visit the Monticello gift shop and buy giant nickels for the kids. The gift shop has its own small museum. In it a scatter of failed inventions and the ivory diary Jefferson wiped clean each week. *The Cherokees, for example, have formed their language not by single words, but by phrases. I have known some children*

learn to speak, not by a word at a time, but by whole phrases. Thus the Cherokee has no name for father in the abstract

In some old paintings, a penciled gesture is just now rising up through varnished sky. The curators retype the interpretive cards: *Pentimenti of an earlier arm can be seen.* A discarded gesture darkening into sight. Now surfacing, interrupting.

The roll of a hill as if a hand had just uncovered it. Driving past Wilderness Battlefield I see one picnicker, next to the woods where bits of bone keep surfacing. The general was called the Meat Grinder for how he pressed the men forward. Yeats said little should be written of war except long afterward; otherwise the entrails distract. Empty roads

against trees whose leaves are just turning. Turning, we say, though the flash of color has waited beneath all year. Under green, pressing up.

In Jefferson's reading room (more stairs than books), a lucky few wear cotton gloves. Not me, today, subsisting on copies. Each of our searches recorded, shelved. By wilderness we no longer mean *the will of the land*. Instead, more blank vocabularies ready for the field. Here and there a mineral shadow.

Brother			
Sister			
the body			
the hair			
the breast			
the face			
Summer			
Autumn			
Winter			
a man			
a day			

Mother gardens, Jefferson called his beds, full of fruit he
hadn't named yet. But what of those who resisted his graft?
Oranges rolling loose under my seat, I miss the turn twice,
three times. Jefferson left no room on his vocabularies for
grammar. Imagine the bones of your language rearranged,

some extra.

I'm staying overnight in an old plantation house, broken now into apartments. My bedroom half the size of the bathroom, where the tub drain has lost its seal. The woman running the place is divorced and sells coffee mugs with grammar jokes printed on the side. I try the drain myself;

I used to be able to do this. Outside the fields go on as far as I can see. There is a wraparound porch to watch from. To watch the work, at first, making sure it got done right. To take the subjects out of sentences, to leave them in the field. To expect a harvest. To enter the borrowed field.

This field is far from empty and it is not mine to enter. Along these soft hills, along this shallow crooked river, both men and languages were once collected. One of the men walks out of the field toward the river.

THOMAS JEFFERSON TO BENJAMIN SMITH BARTON
Monticello, September 21, 1809

Dear Sir,

                                        thirty years

            of the Indian vocabularies

        the whole

the thief
                        the river
                        of which he thought

        some leaves floated ashore & in the mud

I turned to them
                        very happy

                                only morsel   *Lewis'*

        & a little fragment of some other

                                                as

can ever be made of the wrecks of my loss

May 30, 1809, in the *Richmond Examiner*, a \$20 reward offered. Mister Jefferson's 29 trunks from the Capitol and now one missing, no list of what it held. All those ideas he hadn't gotten down yet, down the Potomac to the Chesapeake and up the James. Then, from the canal basin, trunk #29 carried off, poled upriver, pried open:

And contained principally writing paper of various qualities, but also some other articles of stationary, a pocket telescope with a brass case, a Dynanometer in steel and brass, or instrument for measuring the exertions of draught animals, a collection of vocabularies of the Indian languages & some other articles not particularly noted

Microfilm, riverbank. The librarians won't bring out the oldest maps. It's near closing time and they want to go home. I follow the words past the canal basin where Jefferson's boat sat docked, the watchman too friendly. Out to the riverbank. I'm joined by a group of white women whose dogs bark and pull. Tonight they're seeing a psychic. What's gone is gone, says one. You never know

what you're looking at, says another. Nearly dark and every trail unmarked, the flap of a leaf caught in the throat of roots.

Poled along.

[*without our having previously collected and deposited in* **the records of literature** *the general rudiments of at least the languages they spoke*] [*He was furnished with a number of printed vocabularies of the same words and form I had used, with* **blank spaces for the Indian** *words. He was very attentive*] [*I treated them with great distance*] [*impossible to translate our language into any of the Indian, or any of theirs into ours*] [*a collection of vocabularies of the Indian languages, & some other articles not particularly noted*] [*a Noted Villain*] [*he Threw it, with the Balance of the articles overboard, just below Britains Landing, nearly opposite westham*] [*my fear of the original papers relative to my voyage falling into the hands of the British*] [*I am extremely anxious to possess specimens—no matter how small,—of the languages which Mr. Lewis met with*] [*some leaves floated ashore & in the mud*] [*I turned to them*] [*better than will ever occur again to any person having the same desire*] [*I assure you, and I beg you, Sir, to assure his friends*]

I have so many folders open the librarian hovers. 4. *may call silver* white flame, *the very name, I would observe, which the [Mahoxpe?] & same as the neighboring tribe give to this [3 words illegible]—But all these arguments may ultimately be found of no weight or importance, and ten or*

Outside the philosophical society, someone's making a movie. It's not of this.

Left blank: *wind, the cheek, nipple, the mammoth, buffalo, elk, wolf, panther, moose, monax, swan, gold, silver, copper, lake, sycamore, elm, birch,* [in place of *sorrow* he writes *I am sorry*], *weak, he, she, they. This* and *that* are the same.

to part asunder
to join together
to join with a party that you meet out

Stony precision and light. A labyrinth mown into wheat. Each stalk constellates. The wind moves through them. They are barely knee-high: here's me trying to pocket each prickled asterisk.

The genealogists at the Richmond library know how to keep the microfilm rudder from spinning out. At their speed the news blurs. How do they go this fast? I roll through months of handwritten court records, lose the spool and start again. Days now since I called home. I am far inside this story, I cradle it: all the words in one basket, the basket

taken. *No use can ever be made of the wrecks of my loss.* From letters at Monticello I know the theft was at the start of a hot summer. Richmond blistering in the wake of a massive, failed slave revolt. I spool through June, July—

Here. In 200-year-old cursive. *Defendant: Couch's Ned.*

<u>*Burnt*</u> written in the margin.

> *In a court of oyer and terminer Doth order that he be burnt in the left hand and receive thirty nine lashes on his bare back at the public whipping post*

At a conference one poet warned me against having a story to tell. It's not a poem, she said, if it's carrying a burden. *nothing can ever be made.* As a girl I once sank a boy's letters in a jar of water, and gradually what he'd said went blank, tinting the water blue. *I believe we shall find it impossible to translate our language into any of the Indian, or any*

of theirs into ours   But the vocabularies are listed among Lewis's effects, three months after Ned was burned and whipped. Then shipped to Philadelphia, to a self-taught pediatrician who took them in, so curious, his desk *an immence heap* of fevers and ideas. Linguistic theories scrawled on the back of medical notes. *Mrs. Gumphert has tried to*

give him suck in the cradle but he wont take it & likewise it is impossible   No page leads to another, the big book never gotten to, the Indian vocabularies neither here nor there. How long does the blankness take if there is no water in the jar.

By blankness I mean whiteness, I mean the distance. The fog. The idea that distance is a thing you can have. I mean I live in Seattle now. I have a newcomer's love of the fog, the bristled shore. Out west the ocean is firm against a wall of cedar, but back east: back east is that long idle beach where you think you can see forever. Back east is where I am from.

At the new Museum of the American Indian, running
late, I dragged the kids straight to the information desk.
What have you got I said on the vocabularies or at least the
Chinook? My kids spun out down the hall. We're not laid
out like that, the man said. We have our own stories to tell.

Loosed from record, the vocabularies are everywhere by now, in the river, in an attic, in the air. They have colored the water. Vowels cracked open, licked free of names and loves. Or carried inside the body. Swallowed. Because these words resist me does not mean they are lost. I can't seem to keep to the path, though again and again a sign

says *path*. The maples are red, yellow, everything, slurring sky and lawn. A groundskeeper passes on a riding mower herding the leaves, parsing lawn, tree, road, rock. The year compiled, carried off. Back in the archive: a twentieth-century Pawnee voice recording of an old man stumbling as he tells a story that no one has translated. *Wait,* he

interrupts himself, *wait for a minute.* You can't say Lewis's vocabularies are lost, the librarian says as I return my last cart of files. Only that you haven't found them.

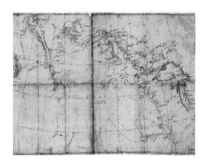

"No general use can ever
be made of the wrecks of my loss"

A Reconsidered History of the Indian Vocabularies Collected on the Lewis and Clark Expedition[1]

Hoping comparative linguistics would prove that Native languages descended from European or Asian roots, Thomas Jefferson collected dozens of Indian vocabularies from 1791 until the early 1820s, lamenting that so many Native tribes had disappeared "without our having previously collected and deposited in the records of literature the general rudiments at least of the languages they spoke."[2]

Jefferson created his own template for the vocabularies: an oversize printed cardstock sheet that folds into quadrants for travel, with constellations of related English words beginning with *fire* and ending with *no*. There is room next to each of the 280 English words for recording a Native equivalent, but no room on the page for any context: no space for any of those who gathered vocabularies on his behalf to write down contextual notes about the people or the community, and no room for notes on grammar. By the time the Corps of Discovery set out, Jefferson had twenty-two Indian vocabularies, gathered from tribes east of the Mississippi. With the help of a number of amateur collectors, that collection eventually grew to thirty or forty Indian vocabularies from the eastern tribes.

When he sent Meriwether Lewis and William Clark on their 1804–1806 journey, Jefferson asked them to collect Indian vocabularies, and they did so, compiling vocabularies of at least twenty-three Native languages, many of these from tribes west of the Mississippi whose words had never before been recorded in written form. Lewis sent two word lists (from the Iowa and the Lakota) back with Captain Amos Stoddard, and another nine back from St. Louis in the fall of 1806. Lewis brought the remaining ten to twelve vocabularies to Jefferson in person at the end of the expedition. After showing the vocabularies to the president and likely allowing them to be copied, Lewis asked Jefferson for permission to keep his originals so that he might publish them along with his journals and scientific findings. In a spring 1807 prospectus for his planned publication, Lewis states that the second volume of the account "will contain a comparative view of twenty three vocabularies of distinct Indian languages, procured by Captains Lewis and Clark on the voyage."[3]

And yet the vast majority of these Indian vocabularies, and the rest of Jefferson's, were never published. The brief period of intense European-American interest in Native languages, during which many Indian vocabularies were collected by amateur fieldworkers hoping to capture what they perceived to be the last echoes of a disappearing civilization, gave way to a scholarly silence.

While president, Jefferson often traveled between the White House and the home he was building at Monticello, shipping dozens of trunks of his possessions. These trunks traveled by boat from the Washington D.C. down the Potomac River to the Chesapeake Bay and up the James River to Richmond, Virginia, and then were transferred to smaller boats for the last leg of their journey up one of the two private canals on Jefferson's Monticello estate.

Losses were not uncommon. On June 4, 1807, several months after Meriwether Lewis published his prospectus, Jefferson wrote to Lewis of the loss of animal artifacts the explorers had collected: "The horns, which I could not take on with me, were packed into one of 25 boxes, barrels, &c. which I sent round by water.

The vessel was stranded, and everything lost which water could injure."[4] In his reply of June 27, Lewis writes, "I sincerely regret the loss you sustained in the articles you shiped for Richmond; it seems peculiarly unfortunate that those at least, which had passed the continent of America and after their exposure to so many casualties and wrisks should have met such destiny in their passage through a small portion only of the Chesapeak."[5]

The incident of loss that has been linked to the Indian vocabularies collected by Lewis and Clark took place in the spring of 1809, as Jefferson ended his presidential term and left the capital for the last time. Jefferson's boat, loaded with twenty-nine trunks, waited overnight in Richmond, in the James River Canal basin, anchored near Pickets Lumber Yard and watched over by an unnamed boatman. In the early morning hours, one of the trunks was stolen. Jefferson hadn't made an inventory of the trunks' contents, but over the next few weeks he created a list of what was missing. On June 16, his cousin George placed an advertisement in the Richmond Enquirer, seeking information about a trunk that had "contained principally writing paper of various qualities, but also some other articles of stationary, a pocket telescope with a brass case, a Dynamometer in steel and brass, or instrument for measuring the exertions of draught animals, a collection of vocabularies of the Indian languages, & some other articles not particularly noted in the memorandum taken."[6]

In a July 1809 letter to George Jefferson from Samuel J. Harrison,[7] a local tobacco merchant and Lynchburg alderman, it appears that Jefferson had asked Harrison to carry a search for the thief. Harrison accuses Ned, "a Noted Villain," and a slave owned by the recently deceased James B. Couch of Buckingham County, of the theft. According to Harrison, "he Threw it, with the Balance of the articles overboard, just below Britains Landing, nearly opposite westham."[8]

In Richmond, enslaved men and women worked in town, typically dividing their hours between labor for the family who owned them and additional hours for other families on a seasonal or as-needed basis, sometimes living independently and/ or taking meals in town. Slave owners commonly protected each others' vested interest in this interconnected system by refraining from crippling, killing, imprisoning, or otherwise impacting the work potential of each others' enslaved workers.[9] Ned's uncertain status in the wake of Couch's death would likely not have gone unnoticed during the search for a suspect. Prosecuting Ned would cause minimal, if any, problems for members of the Richmond slave-owning community.

On July 25, 1809, in Richmond, Virginia, a closed court of oyer and terminer was convened to hear the case.[10] Thomas Jefferson was not present at the trial, which lasted less than a day. Here is my transcription of the sole piece of evidence filed, a letter handwritten by Richmond mayor John Lynch Jr.:

> Whereas H. Parrington of the corporation aforesaid hath given information, this day upon oath, to me John Lynch Jr. mayor of said corporation, that he is advised by George Jefferson of the City of Richmond, that on or about the [space left blank] day of [space left blank] last past at or near the City of Richmond, there was feloniously taken, stolen, and carried away from on Board a Certain Batteau, the property of [space left blank] then [2 words illegible] the city of Richmond, the Canal locks, a certain trunk, the property of Thomas Jefferson Esquire [. . .] was taken, stolen, & carried away by Ned, a Negro man slave, the property of the Estate of James B. Couch, dec'd, late of the County of Buckingham, [illegible] are therefore in the name of the Commonwealth [illegible] to apprehend the slave Ned, & to bring him before me, to answer the premises & further to be dealt with according to law—Given and in my hand this 13th day of July 1809.

The evidence was mainly hearsay: George Jefferson told H. Parrington who swore to John Lynch Jr. that Ned was the thief. Lynch found Ned "guilty of felony and doth order that he be burnt in the left hand and receive thirty nine lashes on his bare back at the public whipping post."[11]

This petty theft, a felony: a harsh conviction even by the standards of slave courts, but indicative of the climate of white fear in Richmond at that time. Nine years earlier, hundreds of black men and women, enslaved and freed, had nearly carried out a violent citywide insurrection against slave-owning families known as Gabriel's Revolt. In the wake of that near-revolution, white citizens put in place stricter laws governing the mobility of both enslaved and freed blacks in Richmond, with brutal punishments for the smallest infractions.

It is unclear whether Meriwether Lewis, living in Louisiana at the time, heard about the incident in which Jefferson's Indian vocabularies were thrown overboard into the James River. Lewis hadn't yet published his journals from the expedition, nor any of his Indian vocabularies, and that summer he became increasingly anxious about the risk of his papers falling into the wrong hands. In September 1809, Lewis embarked on a trip to Washington D.C. in hopes of resolving some of his ongoing personal financial problems, and then to Philadelphia to deliver expedition-related papers to the publisher who had agreed to bring out the work. Lewis had initially planned to travel by water, but then decided the river route was too dangerous, and so traveled by land through the Chickasaw Nation, stating in a letter to President James Madison dated September 16, 1809, "My apprehension from the heat of the lower country and my fear of the original papers relative to my voyage falling into the hands of the British has induced me to change my rout and proceed by land through the state of Tennisee to the City of washington."[12]

Waiting in Philadelphia was Benjamin Smith Barton, a linguist and self-credentialed pediatrician, who has been portrayed as both Jefferson's collaborator and competitor. Jefferson and Barton shared an interest in Native languages, and often swapped records in the mail so that one could make a copy of the other's vocabularies. When I examined their papers, I had the sense of two men with very different approaches to the work. Where Jefferson's handwriting is tiny, precise, and upright, Barton's is loose, scrawled, barreling forward. Jefferson recorded an exhaustive catalog of his daily life and observations in carefully bound logbooks, while Barton wrote on loose scraps of paper, including the verso of his medical notes. Trying to follow Barton's notes from one scrap to the next is a daunting, gap-filled task, and one has the sense of a man continually interrupted or distracted.

Barton had helped to train Meriwether Lewis in the practice of collecting Indian vocabularies. Barton wrote to Jefferson on September 14, 1809, with the news that he was about to publish a book on American Indian languages, stating, "I am extremely anxious to possess specimens—no matter how small,—of the languages which Mr. Lewis met with beyond the Mississippi. I will think myself much gratified, and honoured, if you will transmit to me, as early as your convenience may suit, such specimens."[13]

Jefferson, in his September 21 reply, described the thirty years he had dedicated to amassing a comprehensive collection of about fifty Indian vocabularies, a period during which he says that his "opportunities were probably better than will ever occur again to any person having the same desire."[14] By the time of the May 1809 theft of his trunk, however, Jefferson had not published or even fully studied the vocabularies he possessed, and so when the bulk of his collection was dropped into the river that day, an irreplaceable set of records was lost. As Jefferson observes in his letter to Barton,

> Some leaves floated ashore & were found in the mud; but these were very few, & so defaced by the mud & water that no general use can ever be made of them. On the receipt of your letter I turned to them, & was very happy to find that the only morsel of an original vocabulary among them was Capt Lewis's of the Pani language of which you say you have not one word. I therefore inclose it to you, as it is, & a little fragment of some other, which I see is in his handwriting, but no indication remains on it of what language it is. [. . .] altho I believe no general use can ever

be made of the wrecks of my loss, yet I will ask the return of the Pani vocabulary when you are done with it. perhaps I may make another attempt to collect, altho' I am too old to expect to make much progress in it. . . . [15]

Jefferson had copied Lewis's vocabularies before Lewis took them back, so the "Pani" Jefferson mentions would likely have been a copy of Lewis's Pawnee vocabulary washing up, not the original.

Three weeks later, early in the morning of October 11, 1809, having only made it as far as Nashville, Meriwether Lewis shot himself. In the Memorandum of Lewis's Personal Effects[16] dated November 23, "one do. vocabulary" is listed, with the note that this document was forwarded on, with all other items relating to the expedition, to William Clark, whose responsibility at that point would be to find someone to help write the narrative of the journey, and to prepare his and Lewis's journals for publication in Philadelphia. In an April 6, 1818, letter to American Philosophical Society Historical Committee chair William Tilghman, publisher Nicholas Biddle recalls delivering Indian vocabularies to Benjamin Smith Barton after Lewis's death:

My recollection is not as accurate as it would have been had they fallen more immediately under my examination. My impression however is that [. . .] the papers were Indian vocabularies, collected during the journey. They formed, I think, a bundle of loose sheets each sheet containing a printed vocabulary in English with the corresponding Indian name in manuscript. [. . .] In the preface to the printed travels which, being published in Phila. whilst Dr. Barton was there, must be presumed to have been correct it is stated that "[. . .] the alphabets of the Indian languages are in the hands of Professor Barton, and will it is understood, shortly appear." This was in 1814. I have mentioned these particulars so minutely because their description may perhaps enable some members of the Committee to recognize the vocabularies, which I incline to think were the only things delivered to me by Dr. Barton not included in the volumes now deposited.[17]

In 1810, Barton wrote to Jefferson, "In regard to Mr. Lewis's papers, I assure you, and I beg you, Sir, to assure his friends, that they will be taken good care of; that it is my sincere wish to turn them, as much as I can, to his honour & reputation; and that they shall ultimately be deposited, in good order, in the hands of General Clark, or those of Mr. Conrad, the publisher. During the Governor's [Lewis's] last visit to Philadelphia, there was some difference between him and me."[18]

Barton died in 1815. He did not publish any of Lewis's vocabularies during his lifetime. After his death, his widow blocked access to his study, where one observer described his disorganized desk as "an immence heap."

In a letter dated April 26, 1816, to José Corrèa da Serra (who was soon to become Spanish ambassador to the United States), Jefferson wrote of Lewis's Indian vocabularies,

> I had myself made a collection of about 40. vocabularies of the Indians on this side of the Missisipi, and Capt. Lewis was instructed to take those of every tribe beyond, which he possibly could: the intention was to publish the whole, and leave the world to search for affinities between these and the languages of Europe and Asia. He was furnished with a number of printed vocabularies of the same words and form I had used, with blank spaces for the Indian words. He was very attentive to this instruction, never missing an opportunity of taking a vocabulary. After his return, he asked me if I should have any objection to the printing his separately, as mine was not yet arranged as I intended. I assured him I had no objection; and I am certain he contemplated their publication. But whether he had put the papers out of his own hand or not, I do not know. I imagine he had not: and it is probable that Doctr. Barton, who was particularly curious on this subject, and published on it occasionally, would willingly receive and take care of these papers after Capt. Lewis's death, and that they are now among his papers.[19]

In 1817, Jefferson offered the remains of his Indian vocabularies to the American Philosophical Society, with the acknowledgment that the ones collected by Meriwether Lewis had not yet been returned by Barton's estate.[20]

Why, in the seventeen years after he lost his eastern vocabularies, didn't Jefferson make a stronger effort to retrieve Lewis's vocabularies from the succession of linguists and publishers who apparently held them? Perhaps he had already taken from the vocabularies what he wanted: an answer to the question of whether the tribal languages bore European or Asian roots.[21] When Jefferson began to compare his Indian vocabularies, it likely became obvious to him that not only was his tongue not the father of these languages, but that these indigenous languages showed a diversity and complexity that indicated Native cultures had existed here for a very long time, diverging and merging by turn as cultures do over thousands of years.[22]

As the young United States government began to create the reservation system and other forms of systemic removal of Native people from their lands, U.S. engagement with indigenous languages and cultures sharply waned. One of the ways in which the Corps of Discovery explorers—and generations of white scholars in their wake—have hampered the continuing work of Native language preservation is by neglecting or abandoning these language records without either publishing the field notes or returning the records to Native linguists.

On February 20, 1825, just eighteen months before his death, Jefferson wrote to the linguist John Pickering about the vast differences in the grammars of Native American and European languages, stating, "I believe we shall find it impossible to translate our language into any of the Indian, or any of theirs into ours."[23] I believe that Jefferson found the theft of his trunkful of vocabularies to be a convenient opportunity to wash his hands of a field of study in which he had lost interest. Subsequent scholars have continued to conflate the riverboat theft with the loss of Lewis's Indian vocabularies, obscuring the path for any linguists who might still hold out hope of recovering these documents. Considering how easily I was able to locate significant "new" findings, I would be truly surprised if there is not more to be found, perhaps including the vocabularies themselves, documents that would be invaluable to contemporary Native linguists and historians. These distinctive vocabularies, on oversize card stock, would be unlikely to have ever been mistaken for scrap. A deeper search among Benjamin Smith Barton's papers, or a search among the papers of other amateur linguists with whom Barton exchanged language samples, might be fruitful.

Some of Barton's papers, along with Jefferson's, are held at the American Philosophical Society.[24] Among these documents are Indian vocabularies recorded by amateur compilers, most still unpublished, as well as the carefully archived, mud-stained remnants of the ones retrieved from the James River. Searching every file, I could find no trace of the vocabularies Meriwether Lewis painstakingly collected. That doesn't mean they can't be found. "You can't say that Lewis's vocabularies are lost," archivist Brian Carpenter at the American Philosophical Society reminded me at the end of my three-day search. "It's only that you did not find them."

As a white poet whose recent archival work has ushered me into many small, closed rooms of "findings" stored out of sight in museum attics or library special collections, I feel a responsibility to speak out against the combination of scholarly hoarding and neglect I have encountered, and to try not to perpetuate that mentality in my own work. It is not my place to continue the search for these vocabularies: they are not mine to find. Whether or not those particular Indian vocabularies are ever located, I hope that this part of the story might be of use to Native scholars and linguists, and that a correction of the historical account will encourage Lewis and Clark historians to engage the questions raised here, rather than portray this story as closed.

Notes

1. I use the term "Indian vocabularies" as a historically significant marker when referring to the written lists of Native equivalents for common English words recorded by white Americans in the late eighteenth and early nineteenth centuries. In this examination of scholarly erasure, I don't want to perpetuate erasure myself by rewording any part of this troubling history, or by pretending that the whites who collected, traded, studied, and eventually lost track of these word lists called them anything other than Indian vocabularies. When referring to indigenous peoples or their languages (in contrast to a particular historical set of language records), I use the name of the specific tribe whenever possible, which in this essay is depressingly—tellingly—rare. Now seven years into my research on the Indian vocabularies collected by Lewis and Clark, I still cannot find a clear record of which Native languages, exactly, they catalogued.

2. Thomas Jefferson, *Notes on the State of Virginia* (London: John Stockdale, 1787), 164.

3. Reuben Gold Thwaites, ed., *Original journals of the Lewis and Clark Expedition, 1804–1806* (New York: Dodd, Mead & Co., 1904), Appendix.

4. Donald Jackson, ed., *Letters of the Lewis and Clark Expedition: With Related Documents 1783–1854* (Champaign: University of Illinois Press, 1962), 415.

5. Ibid., 418.

6. "Reward Offered," *The Enquirer* (Richmond, Virginia), May 30, 1809: 4. Accessed via microfiche November 2012.

7. Samuel J. Harrison (1771–1846) was a tobacco merchant who had served as a Lynchburg alderman since the Virginia

town's 1805 incorporation. In 1810, Jefferson sold him two land parcels along Ivy Creek. See Ruth H. Early, "*Campbell Chronicles and Family Sketches,*" *Embracing the History of Campbell County, Virginia, 1782–1926* (Lynchburg: J. P. Bell Company, 1927), 63–64; and James A. Bear Jr. and Lucia C. Stanton, eds., *Jefferson's Memorandum Books: Accounts, with Legal Records and Miscellany, 1767–1826* (Princeton: Princeton University Press, 1997), 2: 1254–56.

8. Barbara B. Oberg and J. Jefferson Looney, eds., *The Papers of Thomas Jefferson Digital Edition* (Charlottesville: University of Virginia Press, Rotunda, 2008).

9. My understanding of Richmond's slavery system is largely thanks to Midori Takagi's careful and nuanced study, *Rearing Wolves to Our Own Destruction: Slavery in Richmond, Virginia 1782–1865* (University of Virginia Press, 2002).

10. Richmond, Library of Virginia, Richmond Hastings Court Suit Papers 1809: Box 13, BC 1007262 and Box 14, BC 1007261. Accessed November 2012.

11. Ibid.

12. Donald Jackson, ed., *Letters of the Lewis and Clark Expedition: With Related Documents 1783–1854* (Champaign: University of Illinois Press, 1962), 464.

13. Ibid., 463–64.

14. Ibid., 465–66.

15. Ibid., 465–66.

16. Ibid., 470–72.

17. Ibid., 635–36.

18. Ibid., 561–62.

19. Ibid., 611–13.

20. Ibid., 631–33.

21. Edward G. Gray, *New World Babel: Languages and Nations in Early America* (Princeton: Princeton University Press, 2014), 127–32.

22. Andrew H. Fisher, *Shadow Tribe: The Making of Columbia River Indian Identity* (Seattle: University of Washington Press, 2010).

23. Oberg and Looney, eds., *The Papers of Thomas Jefferson Digital Edition.*

24. "Benjamin Smith Barton papers," B B284.d, Series II: Subject Files, Indian Materials. American Philosophical Society, Philadelphia. Accessed November 2012.

Acknowledgments

Thanks to the editors of the following journals where
these pieces first appeared, many in earlier versions.

Cincinnati Review: "Clark at Cape Disappointment"

City Arts: [where is my love where is his phone cord . . .]

Crab Creek Review: "Pastoral"

Ecotone: "The Indian Vocabularies"

Image: "Guide to Avian Architecture," "Hive Paths"

King County/4Culture's Poetry on the Buses: [To create
the distance a frontier demands . . .]

Poetry Northwest: "Abundance," "Sandy (Quicksand) River"

The Southern Review: "The Skelleton of this monster on the Sand"

*Wicazō Sa: "No General Use Can Ever Be Made of the Wrecks
of My Loss"*

Witness: "Ozette"

"The Skelleton of this monster on the Sand" was composed in
November 2009 at locations along the Columbia River near the
site of Lewis and Clark's November 1805 arrival at the Pacific
and the site of their 1805–1806 winter camp, with the support
of an Individual Artist grant from the 4Culture Foundation and
a residency at Willapa Bay AiR. All italicized quotations in this
sequence are taken from *The Definitive Journals of Lewis and Clark*

in seven volumes (University of Nebraska Press, 2002), edited by Gary E. Moulton.

At the Experimental Forest was composed primarily in November 2011 during a residency at the H. J. Andrews Experimental Forest in Oregon, as part of their Long-Term Ecological Reflections study.

The Indian Vocabularies was composed primarily in November 2012 at Monticello, the Monticello Library, and the Library of Virginia; on the banks of the James River where (or near where) scraps of the stolen vocabularies washed up; and at the American Philosophical Society, the Pendle Hill Quaker Retreat Center, and the National Museum of the American Indian. Italicized quotations in this section are taken primarily from the papers of Thomas Jefferson and Benjamin Smith Barton relating to their study of Indian vocabularies, archived at the American Philosophical Society, and from original court and newspaper files stored at the Library of Virginia. Transcriptions are my own except in the case of Jefferson's and Lewis's letters, which have been published as cited in the Notes.

I am grateful for all of the support, education, and discussion that helped to shape my research and writing these past six years. So many people gave generously of their time and expertise.

Thanks to archivists and librarians at the American Philosophical Society, Lewis & Clark College, the University of Washington, the Library of Virginia, the Jefferson Library, Harvard University's Peabody Museum of Archaeology and Ethnology, the Makah Cultural and Research Center, and the National Museum of the American Indian, with particular gratitude to Brian Carpenter at APS and Anna Berkes at Monticello.

For the gifts of space and time, I'm grateful to the 4Culture Foundation for an Individual Artist grant, and to the Helen Riaboff Whiteley Center, Willapa Bay AiR, Pendle Hill, and the H. J. Andrews Experimental Forest for residencies. And grateful to the grandmas and babysitters who watched the kids while I worked: Carol Lehman, Clarena M. Snyder, Becky Jo Tuell Simpson, Virginia Whalen, and Roxanne Rappaport. And thank you to my kids, who helped make space for me to do this work.

For patient and thoughtful early readings, I am grateful to Bill Bevis, Elizabeth Bradfield, Martha Collins, Laura Da', Darcie Dennigan, John M. Findlay, Sonia Greenfield, Jessica Johnson, Meredith Lewis, Erin Malone, Melinda Mueller, Rachel Richardson, Isabelle Grizzard Robertson, Jesse Robinson, David Roderick, Laura Shoemaker, Martha Silano, Sarah Steinke, and Sara Wainscott. Erin Malone, in particular, read each of these pieces as they were first written, and sat with the manuscript again and again as I shaped it into a book. Thanks also to Elizabeth Austen, Randy Barker, Linda Bierds, Suzanne Bottelli, Bill Carty, Christine Deavel, Natalie Diaz, Katy Didden, Soren Eberhardt, Cyndy Hayward, Joan Naviyuk Kane, Kate Koester, Frances McCue, John Marshall, Ben Pennington, Katie Peterson, Jeff Smith, Elissa Washuta, and Suzanne Wynne for critical conversations and reading lists. And to Cara Blue Adams at *The Southern Review* and Anna Lena Phillips Bell at *Ecotone*, two incredibly generous editors in conversation with whom the scope of the book's two long sequences grew much clearer. And to Jim Schley, Jeffrey Levine, Marie Gauthier and the whole Tupelo crew for believing in this work and shepherding it all onto the printed page.

TJ, I am so grateful for your roadside patience and history-buff impatience.

Other Books from Tupelo Press

See our complete list at www.tupelopress.org